Dear Walter. Thought you
would appreciate his
donation especially
now, while in hospital.

Annie

ETHER AND ME

OR

"Just Relax"

BY

WILL ROGERS

Pictures by Grim Natwick

NEW YORK · LONDON

G. P. PUTNAM'S SONS

The Knickerbocker Press

1929

Made in the United States of America

ETHER AND ME

OR

"JUST RELAX"

ETHER AND ME

HERE'S a fact that might interest you:
This is a yarn about a suffering Actor.

Now I knew a man that always sub-
scribed for the Congressional Record. It,
of course, mentioned the fact if any Member of Congress had passed away. So he
said he always took it because he just
loved to read about dead Congressmen.
Oftentimes you have been made to suf-
fer by Actors. So you will be tickled to
death to read about an Actor who suffers,

and the more continuous he suffers, the more you will like it.

Now Irvin Cobb—bless his ugly old frontispiece—not only gave us many a laugh with his classical Operation Book but he showed us the practical side of humor by making an operation pay its way.

'Course Cobb could do it on his, and maybe Bernard Shaw might if the operation was only a shave. But if mine's not humorous, why, don't blame me. It's hard to be funny when you know the check will only pass through your hands.

We kid about our Doctors and we hate to pay 'em after it's all over and we have quit hurting. But I expect a lot of us have got 'em to thank for being here. So I dedicate both check and book to two charming members of an ancient and—I hope—honorable craft—Drs. Percy G. White, and Clarence E. Moore. Don't be misled by their effeminate given names. They are a couple of big rough bruisers, physically.

This story opens on the bank of the Verdigris River in the good old Indian Territory, four miles east of a town called Oo-lo-gah, and twelve miles north of a town called Claremore—best Radium water in the World. The plot of the story is a pain in the stomach. The stomach was located amidships of a youth who was prowling up, down, in and across said Verdigris River.

The plot first appeared when the stomach was at a tender and growing age. It would generally appear after too many green apples, too many helpings of navy beans, of which said stomach has always been particularly fond, and right after hog-killing time. With the back-bones and the cracklins and chitlins, the old plot would bob up again.

As I think back on it, we were a primitive people in those days. There were only a mighty few known diseases. Gunshot wounds, broken legs, toothache, fits, and anything that hurt you from the lower end of your neck on down as far as your hips was known as bellyache. Appendicitis would have been considered as the name of a new dance or some new game with horseshoes. Gallstones would have struck us as something that the old-time Gauls would heave at the Philistines or the Medes and the Persians—maybe get up on Mount Mussolini and roll them down on 'em.

Nervous indigestion was another unknown quantity. In order to have it you had to be nervous and in order to be nervous you had to imagine you had some imaginary illness and that nobody understood you.

Well, in those days, when you felt that way and couldn't explain why you were queer, why, they had an asylum for you. There was no such thing as indigestion then, as everybody worked. Of course, when a bunch was talking and there was quite a sprinkling of girls and women, why, we did have such a parlor name for this plot as Cramp Colic; that was the Latin for bellyache.

I don't remember when I first had it, but I sure do remember one of my dear old Mother's remedies for it. They just built a fire in the old kitchen stove and heated one of the old round flat kitchen stove lids—the thing you take off the stove if you want what you're cooking to burn. Well, they would heat it up—not exactly red hot, but it would be a bright bay. They took it off, wrapped it up in something and delivered it to your stomach with a pair of tongs.

We didn't know what a hot-water bottle was, and the only thing made out of rubber then was boots and the top of lead pencils and gents' wearing collars. A drug store had to get their money then out of paregoric, Cheatam's Chilli Tonic and pills by subscription. There were no rubber goods, banana splits, steaks, lettuce sandwiches, flivvers and flasks. In those

days a rolling pin was made to flatten out a pan of biscuits and not to flatten out the starches in a protruding stomach.

Well, the heat from one of those stove lids burned you so you soon forgot where you were hurting. It not only cured you but it branded you. You would walk stooped over for a week to keep your shirt from knocking the scab off the parched place. Anybody that would look at you who was not familiar with a stove cap would think that an elephant had stepped on you. All it needed was the little scalloping around the edges to make it look like where his toes had sunk in.

After a little spell of this the plot maybe wouldn't show up for a year or maybe two years. Well, a little thing like that didn't compose much sickness for a strong-bodied and weak-minded old boy to have. Having a cramp colic every two or three years didn't hardly bring me under the heading of what you would call a invalid.

Oh, yes, I did have some chills, too, one summer, from what we afterwards learned was malaria. I used to have one every other day. Some people have them every day, but you can't expect in this world to have everything. Days when there were no chills billed with me I could get out and do a fair Kid's day's work, but on chill days I didn't punch the clock at all. My day's work was to chill, and I hope I am not egotistical in saying it, but I did a good job at it. I had it down pat.

This is the way you chill: First you get cold and you shake, your teeth chatter and your body commences shimmying. It's the same thing Gilda Gray got and never got over. Only she was smart enough to cash in on it. City folks call it a dance; we call it a disease. Then after the shaking is over you get a fever and your head hurts like it is going to bust. When the head quits hurting and the fever goes away, why, that's all there

11

is to the chill; it's over—that is, it's over
for that day.

I used to try to have them two days
running so that would give me a few days

off; but, no sir, you couldn't do it, those
chills knew when they were going to happen and they happened. If you get chills
that is working right, you can make a bet
on when it is going to happen. A lot of

people in those days who had chilling children didn't have to keep a clock or a calendar. If Lizzie had a chill early in the week you'd know it was ten o'clock

Monday morning. Quinine was a regular food, not a medicine. It set on the table the same as sugar. The minute you would take it you'd eat something right quick to take away the taste, but you never could do it quick enough.

Well, I finally shook the chills off and in years to come I never was bothered with them any more. But the old plot of the piece, the stomach ache, she would play a return date about every couple of years. I had it here in the movies one day when I was working, and they put a mustard

plaster on it, as there was no such thing as a stove cap in Hollywood. They had all been replaced by the can opener. Well, with this plaster on my stomach, I un- consciously did the funniest scene I ever did in my life. It was in a picture called Jubilo.

Well, to go on with the plot. It hadn't shown up in years, until one spring, on my tour of national annoyances, I hit a town called Bluefield, West Virginia. I hadn't been there long when the old plot showed up. Now ordinarily when a pain hits you in the stomach in Bluefield, West Virginia, you would take it for gunshot wounds. But the old town has quieted down now and the sharpshooters have all joined the Kiwanis and Rotary Clubs. So I knew it wasn't wounds. Then the pain struck me before the nightly lecture and I knew no one would shoot me before the lecture, unless by chance he had heard it over in another town.

Well, the next time it hit me was just a few weeks later, out at my old ranch on the Verdigris River, in the same house where I was born and where I had previously balanced those flat irons on my stomach years before. My niece, who was living there and had a baby, she gave me some asafetida. The only thing it tastes like is spoiled onions and overripe garlic mixed. And the longer after you have taken it, the worse it gets. If I was a baby and I found out that somebody had given me that, if it took me forty years to grow up, I would get them at the finish, even if it was my mother.

Just a few nights after that, and my last night on the train coming home to check up on the moral conditions of Beverly and Hollywood, the Sodom and Gomorrah of the West, that night the old pain hit me again. You see, the plot is slowly thickening. Instead of quitting

me after a few hours, as it generally had,
it kept hanging on. If it did go away, it
would be right back.

When I got home they called in a doctor. He gave me some powders. The
pain just thrived on those powders. I
never saw a pain pick up so quick as it
did when the powder hit it. Instead of
setting around like most people do, I
would take a stool or chair and arrange
myself over it something like this: My
head and arms would be on the floor on
one side and my knees and feet on the
floor on the other side. My middle was
draped over the seat of the chair.

Finally my wife called in Doctor
White, a famous physician. He had as-
sisted us in some other family illnesses
and we knew his telephone number. Well,
he came and he had one of those old-

time phonograph tubes where you stick
one end in each ear, hold the other up
against your chest and see what you can
get. The static must have been something

terrible, because he pulled it away and
shook his head. I thought maybe that he
had found out that I wasn't breathing and
didn't know it. Then he would lay his
hand on my stomach and thump the back

part of his own hand with his other one. That formed a kind of contact and gave him sort of a new connection—or a wave length.

"What part of your stomach hurts?" he asked.

"Practically all of it, Doc."

I almost forgot to tell you that the first part he got to thumping and feeling around on was down low on the right-hand side, where I had always been led to believe the appendix is. I says, "There's where you are wrong, Doc; that's the only part that don't hurt." He says, "Are you sure there's no pain there?" "I'm absolutely sure, Doctor." Well, that seemed to kind of lick him. An appendicitis operation within his grasp, and here it was slipping through his hands. He looked kind of discouraged.

But he was a resourceful fellow. He never, like a lot of these other doctors, hung all his clothes on one line. I could see his mind was enumerating other diseases that were not down so low. He commenced moving his thumping and listening around to other parts. He began to take soundings around the upper end of the stomach. When I told him it hurt there, I never had any idea that I was announcing a lead for pay dirt. When I told him where the pain was worse, his face began to brighten up.

Then he turned and exclaimed with a practiced and well-subdued enthusiasm, "It's the Gall Bladder—just what I was afraid of." Now you all know what that word "afraid of," when spoken by a doctor, leads to. It leads to more calls.

Now I had heard of the gall bladder in a kind of indirect way, but I never had given much thought about where it was or what it was doing. He then said, "Look up." And as I looked up he examined the lower parts of my eyes. Then he says, "Yes, it's Gallstones." Then I says, "Doc, are they backed up as far as my eyes?" I asked him. "What do you do for them?"

He didn't answer me direct, but he casually inquired if I had had a good season. I told him that outside of Waxahachie, Texas, Hershey, Pennsylvania, Concord, New Hampshire, and Newton, Kansas, I had got by in paying quantities.

He then says, "We operate." My wife says, "Operate?" And as soon as I came to enough I says, "Operate?"

21

My wife says, "Is there no easier way out?"

Then I showed that the pain had not entirely dulled my intellect. "Yes, is there no cheaper way out? Can't they feed me something heavy to wear out the stones?"

"No," he says. "You will always be bothered. The best way is to go down and have them taken out. . . . Where's the phone?"

I didn't know whether he was going to phone for the knives, the hearse, the ambulance or what. The wife pointed to the phone kind of dumfounded. Why didn't I think of telling him the phone was not working? That would have stalled the thing off a little longer. Well, he phoned for what seemed like a friend, but who afterwards turned out to be an accomplice. These doctors nowadays run in pairs and bunches.

This is a day of specializing, especially with the doctors. Say, for instance, there is something the matter with your right eye. You go to a doctor and he tells you, "I am sorry, but I am a left-eye doctor; I make a specialty of left eyes." Take the throat business for instance. A doctor that doctors on the upper part of your throat he doesn't even know where the lower part goes to. And the highest priced one of all of them is another bird that just tells you which doctor to go to. He can't cure even corns or open a boil himself. He is a Diagnostician, but he's nothing but a traffic cop, to direct ailing people.

The old fashioned doctor didn't pick out a big toe or a left ear to make a life's living on. He picked the whole human frame. No matter what end of you was wrong, he had to try to cure you single-handed. Personally, I have always felt

that the best doctor in the world is the Veterinarian. He can't ask his patients what is the matter—he's got to just know.

Well, after a while I heard a big expensive car coming up our driveway hill. It made it. After years of listening we can tell the calibre of our callers by how many times they have to shift gears on our hill inside the yard. When they make it on high without a shift, we go to the door. On a one-shift noise, we let the maids go—I mean the maid. And on a complete stall, why, everybody ducks and no one is at home. Well, this fellow came up on high and right on upstairs, and they met.

There was a kind of knowing look between them, as good as to say, "I think we can get him."

This new one was Dr. Clarence Moore, the operating end of the firm. He is the most famous machete wielder on the Western Coast. He asked the same line of questions, but before I could get a chance to answer them myself, why, Doc White answered them for me the way they should be answered, to show that I had a very severe case of Gallstones. Right away this guy asked about the pain down around that old appendix, but the other one answered him with rather a sigh, "No, it's not there; but I have discovered a better place for it."

It seems the appendix is always their first shot. The first doctor said, "What do you think?" The second one says, "I think Gallstones." The first one says, "That's what I said." I says, "I'm glad you boys are guessing together."

"What do you advise?" the first doctor asked. "I advise an operation," said the second. "That's what I advised," said the first.

Imagine asking a surgeon what he advises! It would be like asking Coolidge, "Do you advise economy?"

My wife said, "When?" The whole thing seemed to have gone out of my hands. I was just lying there marked Exhibit A.

One doctor was for doing it that night, but the next one was more of a humanitarian. He suggested the next morning. Well, Number One rushed to the phone again and called up. I couldn't think who they would be calling now; they already had the doctor and the surgeon.

I says, "The only other man he can possibly work with is the undertaker." But I was relieved to hear that it was only the hospital he was calling. He was asking for a nice room. I heard him say, "Yes, we'll be there in the morning."

My wife says, "Doctor, is there any danger in this operation?" Well, as bad as I felt, I had to laugh at that. They replied together in unison: "Why, there is just about a half of one per cent," as though they had rehearsed it.

I thought, "Those babies have pulled that one many a time. Half of one per cent! That's the chance people have got of taking a drink in this country—is half of one per cent—and look what's happening!"

They were reaching for their hats and all smiling, and you would have thought we had all made a date to have some fun and go hear Aimee preach. They said they would take me down to the hospital and see how I got along.

Well, after the doctors had left, that gave my wife and I a chance to do a little thinking. What they had talked about had scared the pains clear away. We got to wondering what had brought on this severe attack at this time. We laid it to everything we could think of. Will Hays had just been out here and spent the day with us. Now I don't lay the illness directly on to him, but a continual listening to the merits of the Movies and the Republican Party will sometimes react disastrously on a previously ailing stomach.

My wife was setting on the edge of the bed and we were talking it over. She got up and left, and I thought to myself: "Poor Betty, she can't stand this; it's too much for her; she's gone so I can't see her." I got up and went in to console her. She was digging in an old musty leather case marked Insurance Papers.

Well, the household was up bright and early next morning to get old Dad off to the hospital. The whole place was what the novelist would call agog. Even the chauffeur—part time—had the old car shined up. This going to a hospital was a new thing to me. I had never been in one in my life only to see somebody else. Outside of those stove-lid episodes, I had never even been sick a day in my life. I had been appearing on the stage for some twenty-odd years and had never missed a show.

But I was going to make up for it now. They were taking me to the Swedish Lutheran Hospital. I knew nothing about it myself. It didn't make much difference what denomination I was cut under, but the reason we went there was because Lindbergh was at his height then, and I felt like out of respect to him we ought to make it a Swedish year.

We went right in. A hospital is the only place you can get into without having baggage or paying in advance. They don't hold the trunk like a hotel does— they just hold the body.

They had a pretty, cozy room for me. The whole thing was like a big hotel, and I thought I was in the wrong place, because I couldn't smell Iodoform. Everything was jolly and laughter. The stomach had quit hurting, of course. Did you ever have a tooth hurt after you got to the dentist? I couldn't see any use in going to bed at ten o'clock in the morning when I hadn't been out the night before.

Then in came the nurse. Wow! I got one look at her and made it continuous. They introduced her as Miss. She was Ziegfeld's front row without a dissenting

vote. I got one look at Mrs. Rogers, who was looking her over also, and then she says, "Doctor, is this operation necessary?" I spoke up ahead of the doctor

and said, "I'm beginning to think it is."
Then I thought to myself, if this girl is
this good looking and still single, she has
let all her patients die, for if one ever got
out alive they would have nailed onto
her.

Oh, say, I like to forgot to tell you that
during this time I was turning yellow.
One of the symptoms of the gall is that
it produces jaundice.

Well, the doctors were both remarking,
"Very yellow—he is getting yellower."
Ha-ha! They didn't know it, but I
wanted to tell them that that yellow was
from the heart and not from the liver
and gall bladder. They gave instructions
about what to do to get me ready for tomorrow. I didn't think I had anything
to do only just furnish the stomach.
Then I thought maybe the surgeon

wanted to practice a little in the mean-time.

The hilarity was at its height. You'd have thought there was going to be a picnic at the hospital the next day. One thing got me—a great big old hundred-and-eighty-pound lummox having women fussing around him when it didn't seem like he needed them. But later on, I was mighty glad to have them doing something, I tell you. The night nurse was also a very pleasant, cheerful, fine, capable little woman.

Things were going fine now, around the hospital, but up around the old Rogers Igloo things were stirring. The night before the operation, Mrs. Rogers got to studying: "Now these two men just came in here and they say there should be an operation. Of course I know they are fine capable men, the best doctors to be secured on the Western Coast, but I just wish I could get some more advice."

Then she gets hold of Mary Pickford, who lives on the expensive end of the same hill and has a very widely seen house. Betty thinks Mary is mighty smart. In fact, everybody that knows Mary has that same single-track thought. She knew Mary must have a pretty good doctor, for he had been able to keep Doug jumping all these years, and so she thought: "Maybe he can do something for *my* handsome Douglas."

Mary's doctor was out of town. But she knew another one and told my wife about him. She got him. You see, Betty got to thinking, after all the shooting was over, and while I was down in the hospital waiting to be operated on: "Now there's old Will. While he hasn't been a good husband, he's done about the best he could and knew how. While he's been funny to some people he has, at times, been very sad to me. But as ornery as he is, I'm not going to give him up without a struggle."

You see, she had, during our years of association with stage and screen people, seen so many second husbands who hadn't even turned out to be as good as the first that it set her wondering. Then our old friend Bill Hart called up. He had a fine Doctor that he wanted her to talk to and have see me. So she asked our two if they minded her having these other two look me over and all confer.

Well, they of course didn't and they knew it would make her feel better to have more opinions on it, and they felt

their case would stand up before any
witnesses. She made them promise that
they wouldn't operate the next morning
until they had held this foursome over
my fairway.

All the time they were going ahead
getting me all ready. The night before
they wrapped my stomach all up in a ban-
dage. I guess that was so no doctor could
get at it ahead of them. Then there was
a battalion of blood experts.

Every few minutes there would be a
girl come in dressed like a manicurist and
carrying a manicure set. She would say,
"Hold out your left hand." Well, I
wouldn't know whether she was going to
wash it, kiss it, hold it or read it. She
would take a sharp knife and take the
tip end of one finger and cut it and get
the blood and put it in a cute little con-

tainer. I would just get settled down to steady worrying again when in would pop another one. She wanted the same thing only a different finger.

Finally one came in after all the fingers had been tapped, and I said "Good joke on you, there aren't any left." But she kept right on a-coming and grabbed me by the ear, the same way we do when we are going to ear down a bronc to get a hackamore on him. She just slit the lower end of the heavy-set part of my ear. I told her my ear-marks used to be; To crop and split the right and underslope the left. I didn't tell her, though, that we also dewlapped 'em.

I says, "Is there some particular brand of blood that you get from the ear that perhaps wouldn't go in any other locality?" She smiled sweetly, rolled up my ear's blood in a tube and says, "Thank you."

Well, by then I was growing weak from loss of blood. It got so every time a girl would come along with a tray I would start holding out my hands or my ears. I was beginning to think that some of them were keeping a friend who might be anæmic.

The next morning, after what should have been breakfast—but I didn't get any, as they won't operate on a full stomach—in filed the battalion of doctors. Betty was with them. One says, "He is yellow." Then each of the others said, "Yes." One of the new ones would ask a question and before I had a chance to answer, why, one of my original cast would explain in so many fewer words than I could. They listened and they

thumped the same as the first one did.
They discussed it all between themselves.
I, the defendant, wasn't put on the stand
at all. Finally they filed out.

Imagine your life in the hands of a
quartet! I'd rather trust a tenor. I wanted

to get a chance to instruct the jury, but
nothing doing. The clinic was over. The
nurse and I were alone. Betty had gone
out too.

I says, "How long do you think the

jury will be out, and do you think there is any chance of a disagreement?" A hung jury was the best I could hope for. I knew a verdict in my favor was out of the question. I could see by the way they acted that the doctoring profession was a kind of a closed corporation, and while they might be professional rivals, they wouldn't purposely do each other out of anything. I asked the nurse again how she thought things would turn out.

She said, "Oh, they have the operating room engaged; they will have to go through with it now."

"Well," I said, "I had better go ahead then, for I certainly don't want to cancel an operating room. Those people up there are going to be all broken up if I don't come up and be all cut up. But I wonder if there is not someone that would like a nice operation, and I could send them up in my place."

There was a knock on the door and the jury came in. It stood four for operation. In fact five, for poor Betty had been won over with tales of the advantages of a nice neat operation. I knew the minute they opened the door that I had lost, for they all came in a smiling and said, "You are going to feel fine when this is over."

I thought: "Yes, it depends on how I have lived, where I will finish when this is over."

Well, it is customary, I have heard, for the defendant to shake hands with the jury, but that's only in case he's acquitted. They all went out, but forgot to shut the door, and I heard my two bidding the other two goodbye, thanking them and saying, "We'll do as much for you sometime, boys."

My surgeon stepped back into the room with his Vassar graduating gown on. That shows you the verdict was framed beforehand, for they must have had those suits on under their others. Oh, they were tickled to death. If they had been doctor golfers, you would have thought they had broken a hundred and ten. Well, I saw right away they were going to make me a hole-in-one.

The main carver said he had a lot of other operations on that day, but that mine would be first. I asked him if he couldn't take somebody else first—that there might be someone in pain and that I had never felt better in my life. Then I thought his hand might be a little shaky early in the morning.

They put on me a pair of what looked like flannel boots that came pretty nearly up to the knee. They looked like those goloshes that girls wear in the winter and don't fasten the buckles, and when they come down the street they sound like a mule that's running loose with chain harness on. I never did find out what those boots were on me for, unless it was to catch the blood in case I got up and ran out, or to keep me from biting my toe nails in case I got nervous during the operation.

I didn't have any kind of a shirt or nightgown on. I had a sheet kind of draped over me. All I needed was my hands crossed. They tied a white thing around my head. Then all I needed was a Klan card. The doctor had a thing over his mouth so he wouldn't catch the same disease I had.

Bill Hart, bless his old heart, was there. He, like all good sportsmen, wanted to be in at the death. I was on the wagon and all ready. We were waiting signals from the operating room. Betty, God bless her, came over to hold my hand. I told her to go over and hold the surgeon's hand for the next thirty minutes and we would all be safe.

Then we got the signal that we were next. You never saw such hustling around. They seemed to think: "Do you realize there's not a soul in this place being whittled on at this minute?" I bid good-bye to my Betty and the parade started down the hall to the elevator. We passed another wagon with an old boy on it that had just come down. I wondered how he had made it. Then I heard him cussing, and I thought: "He's all right, and even if he passes out, he will have the satisfaction of telling them what he thought of them before he left."

As I was a-rolling to the operating room with my retinue of nurses and doctors as outriders, I thought I ought to pull some kind of a gag when I got in there that would get a laugh. I had never seen one before. The only experience our family had had with operating rooms was when we had the children's tonsils and adenoids removed, which is a juvenile social requirement in Beverly Hills.

There was a kind of a little balcony up above the operating-room floor where people with a well-developed sense of humor could sit and see other people cut up.

It must be loads of fun. But there wasn't a soul in there for my operation. I felt kind of disappointed.

I thought, "Well, here I am maybe playing my last act, and it to an empty house."

There were a lot of doctors and more nurses than I ever saw in my life. One nurse was there they told me afterwards just to count every single thing used inside you during the opening. Every gauze pack and every scissors and knife, no matter how small, has to be checked up and accounted for before any sewing up starts. This removes most of the old-time humor from operations, by making it impossible for anyone to joke about what was left inside them.

One fellow had a kind of a hose with a big nozzle on the end of it. Well, I had by this time thought of my joke and was all ready to pull it and set the whole place in a good natured uproar. I just opened my mouth to utter my comical wheeze when this old hose boy just gently slipped that nozzle right over my mouth and nose both. I wanted to tell him, "Just a minute!" And I started to reach up and snatch it off, and a couple of men who had enlisted as internes, but who in reality were wrestlers on vacation, had me by each hand. I certainly was sore. Here I had this last aspiring wise crack and it had been snuffed out before I could give vent to it. And what made it so bad, I can't think to this day what it was. I remember at the time I thought it was going to be a knock-out, but the gas and the ether completely knocked it into another world.

You see the first thing they bump you off with is gas; that puts you where you won't tell any bum gags. Then they give you the ether; that's the postgraduate course in knock-out drops. When you get that you don't even leave a call.

I knew this old boy was smothering me, but there was nothing I could do about it. After he had kept on a-smothering for a little bit it seemed like another fellow started hammering and drilling a hole through the side of the hospital and kept right on pounding and drilling right towards my head.

Then the birds started singing, but they only sang a minute, when we had a shipwreck and everybody on the boat was going down, and it looked like they were trying to push me under. Then there was a hall full of the craziest looking people.

They would read off some numbers for one man and then some for another, and

then say, "There wasn't enough to nominate." And this same thing went on and on. They were just about to agree, when the world came to an end.

Then a farmer started running and hollering for relief, when somebody shot him to put him out of his mortgages. Another little fellow was a-running and hollering, "I don't choose to run." And all this time I was running faster than anybody. Then I was in a bus trying to make a grade crossing and the bus was crowded with people, and as you know, the trains never run fast until they get near a grade crossing, and they never hit a bus unless it's full.

Well, the train was right on us when the Chinese started shelling the town and saying, "We are Missionaries come to America, and you will have to worship Buddha and go to the Mission schools and learn Chinese." Then the Nicaraguans started dropping airplane bombs on us. We had nothing to do but let them drop. They said, "They wanted to protect the United States, as they wanted to put a canal through here some time."

Then I was rehearsing with the Follies. Coolidge and I were working together. We had an act framed up where we had asked an Englishman to disarm and he started laughing and we couldn't get him stopped, and we had to ring down the curtain.

Then the water kept rising till it got up around the bed and there were women and children and horses and mules and levees and cotton gins and airplanes and boats, and a fellow got up in a big hall in a big city and said, "We can't pass this bill; it will take too much money. If it's passed, the income tax can't be lowered."

Then another crevasse broke and we

were drowning, when I heard the nurse
on one side and my wife on the other
both saying, "Lay perfectly still, you're
all right. You are fine now. Just relax."

How was I going to do anything else?
Wasn't every bone in my body broke?
Wasn't my throat cut? Couldn't I remember falling off a thirty-story build-
ing?

"You'll be all right. Just relax and go
back to sleep. Yes dear, it's all over and
you are fine," said my Betty.

"What's fine? I don't see anything
fine. Didn't the airship burn up and me
right in it?"

"The doctors are right here, dear."

"My Lord, have I got a retake? If
this is what they call saving anybody,
what did they save me for?"

"It's the ether."

"No, it's not the ether; it's me. I know what I'm doing—I'm dying, and you-all are just standing there while I do it. Damn the whole gang of you."

Finally this ether got to leaving me and I sort of remembered what the operation had been for. I asked them, "Did you get any gallstones?" I was interested in the quality and the karats. I thought they might find something unusual, for any stone that hurt me that bad must have had corners on it. I figured it must be a rough diamond.

Yes, they had got some, a couple of sizable dimensions, but nothing in any way approaching what could be used for exhibition purposes. I felt right then that the operation had been a failure. What's the use of having one if you couldn't show something worth crowing about?

I then asked, "Did you take out the Gall Bladder?" He had told me that he might jar me loose from that particular organ.

"No," they said. "We found a condition there that was unusual and it warranted us not taking it out at this time. But we found it, and if at any time you ever have any more trouble with it, why, it will be no trouble to go in and get it."

"Oh," I says, " you found out where it was?" This operation was in the nature of exploration or research. "Well, I'm glad you located it, anyhow; but suppose in my jumping around over the country the way I do, trying to find a Democrat, what if this thing should change its location? It's liable to be here today and gone tomorrow."

I would keep seeing the doctors and nurses coming in and looking down on the floor at the side of my bed. I thought at first it was a dog under the bed. They would frown and look worried and then move away.

I says, "What's under there that's causing all these mysterious peeps?" The nurse said, "That's the drain from the tubes."

"Drain from what tubes?"

"Why, the tubes that the doctors put in your side."

"Why, I thought they opened me up to take out things not to put more in. You talk like there might be a series in there. How many are there, if it's a fair question?"

She looked and counted them and said, "Two."

Two? I was hoping there was more than that. You can never get much distance on one of those two tube sets. We had one at home in Beverly and all we could ever get would be: "Praise the Lord, make it a good collection. God loveth a cheerful giver." It was a woman's voice. I thought: "My goodness, I'm nothing but an old casing with a couple of inner tubes in me."

Well, all this worry of the doctor's was from the fact that I wasn't draining. They had found a rather unusual condition in there. Being in California, it would be unusual. I didn't have sense enough to know it, but I was in pretty bad shape, for this drain was over two days and nights showing up. It seems it wasn't due to defective plumbing, but there was sort of a stoppage in the main duct that comes down out of the liver.

Well, the doctors slept right there at the hospital. They were trying everything from glucose to Murphy's Drip. As bad as I felt, I could tell that something wasn't breaking just right. Things were looking bad for Claremore, Oklahoma's, favorite light-headed comedian. If things didn't show up pretty soon, it looked like I had annoyed my last President. Betty was a better actor than the doctors.

Finally it showed up. Doctor Moore got one look and shouted, "If I was a drinking man I would try some of my own prescriptions tonight." He was so tickled that I believe if I had paid my bill then I would have got fifty per cent off.

He tells me what shape I have been in

and he sits down and takes a card out of his pocket and draws a blue print of the whole thing. That's one thing any Californian can do is draw a blue print showing you where in six months there'll be three banks, a subway and a department store right next to the lot he is trying to sell you.

The main duct—Now I'm going to get into some technical stuff here and it's only people that have had the advantages of superior operations will understand, so the riffraff better skip over this part; it's only for the Intelligentsia. You know there is nothing broadens one like an operation, both mentally and physically. You see, I spoke of duct. Now to you ordinary boneheads, duct is the thing a batter does when a pitcher throws one too close to his bean.

Well, here is what he drew as well as
I can remember: There is a right lobe
and a left lobe of the liver. A good deal
depends on which side the trouble is on.

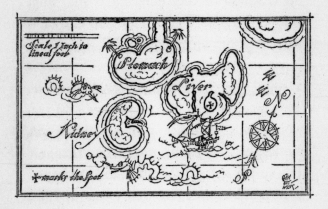

If you eat more on the right side of the
mouth, why, the trouble is likely to be in
the right lobe, and vice versa. The map
started in with the liver, so that was the
North boundary of my trouble. What
laid North or beyond that I have no idea;

it may be the thorax or the medulla ob-
longata.

You know, the liver is shaped kind of
like a boxing glove, and where it's laced
up is where the big duct starts in. Just
below it and sort of around the corner is
what the oil men would call an offset.
Near the termination of the wishbone, is
a small sort of a pocket, or receptacle.
This receptacle is not very large and you
would hardly notice it if it didn't get
stones crossways in its main entrance.
It's called the gall bladder and is shaped
kind of like a hot dog that's been stuffed
more at one end than the other.

Well, this main duct that runs from
the liver South into the stomach runs by
this little hot-dog stand, and there is a
detour line that taps into this miniature
gravel pit. Now it's this little alley that

61

gets clogged up. Of course he had dug it out, but the main duct line above it was the one that wasn't running. No stone would be up there, for a stone won't float uphill.

Well, he explained it so easy I was sorry I hadn't taken up doctoring, for it looked mighty simple. He left me the map. He had written it on the back of a golf score, so I don't know now whether he went from the liver to the main duct in par, or if he took three's on the green. I could tell from the drawings that he was in the rough when he hit the little duct. The drawings looked like he had taken about three niblicks and two putter-mashies to get on the fairway down into the stomach.

Then I would get the nurse to draw what she thought had happened. 'Course she would have the liver on the opposite side and maybe shaped like a bonnet. But I just thought: "If everybody was shaped as different on the inside as they are on the outside, how does a doctor know what part of the body an organ would be located in?"

Take a long tall fellow; his interior furnishings must all be draped up and down, while with a little dumpy, short bird they must lay horizontal. For instance, they must operate on fat people with a sword instead of a knife, and on extremely slender people with a safety razor to keep from going clear through. Take, for instance, the changing waistline of the last few years. Suppose a doctor wanted to reach something directly under a line with it, he wouldn't know whether to lance the lady's shoulder or hip.

Then I had the nurse go to the hospital library and get the doctor books, and we would look at pictures of views taken in this locality, with X marking spot where stones were last seen. These books always showed the interior in colored photography; it looked almost like a Cecil de Mille movie.

Now the Gall goes into this little pocket and remains until needed—that is, until you get sore at somebody and want to use it up on them. That's why it is that good natured people are the ones that have the Gall operations; they never get a chance to use it up on anybody.

Another thing I learned was that the complaint is more common by far among women than among men. Well, that fact didn't please me so much, as I was just bordering on the effeminate as it was. I also learned that it was more prevalent among Jewish people; that's what I get for going to those Kosher restaurants with Eddie Cantor.

Now, as I have so thoroughly and comprehensively explained the location of this, now what causes the stones to form? Well, there are various reasons. Republicans staying in power too long will increase the epidemic; seeing the same ending to Moving Pictures is a prime cause; a wife driving from the rear seat will cause Gastric juices to form an acid, and that slowly jells into a stone as she keeps hollering.

Of course I will always believe that mine was caused by no sanitary drinking cups in the old Indian Territory where I was born. We used a gourd, raised from a gourd vine. Not only did we all drink out of the same gourd but the one gourd lasted for years, till Prohibition weaned some of them away from water.

Then another thing I have thought of recently that might have caused it, which is that our handkerchiefs, when we bought them from the store, were not wrapped in sealed packages. They were just handled in the bulk. Some clerk might have had Gall trouble and slipped it to me in that way. I believe that if modern sanitary methods like the above hadn't come in when they did, that by now four out of five would have had gallstones.

But while lying in the hospital recuperating I just accidentally stumbled on what I really think caused the operation. For years I had carried a very big —that is, big for my circumstances—Accident and Sickness Disability Insurance.

Well, I would notice that my wife would get a little irritable every year when it would come time to pay the premiums on these various sick and accident policies, and say, "Well, that's pretty large to carry, isn't it, when you never have got a cent out of it?" And I would admit it did seem like a bad investment.

It was getting terribly discouraging to keep paying year after year and not being able to get sick, and with no prospects of ever getting sick. Here I was betting a lot of insurance companies that I would get sick or hurt and they were betting me I wouldn't. Now if you think you are not a sucker in a case like that, all you have to do is to look at the financial standing of the company in comparison to the financial standing of the people who bet on the other side. It's just a case of somebody knowing more about you than you know about yourself.

Why, they have the highest priced doctors to look you over. If you look like nothing but lightning can kill you, why, he sends in a report to the company to go ahead and bet you that you won't get sick. But if you look the least bit like you are going to get sick, they don't bet you. Any time they approve of you, that should show you right there that there is nothing going to happen to you. But you, like a fool, go ahead and bet them in the face of all this professional knowledge that you know more than they do.

I argued with my wife, saying, "Well, I may get sick."

"Yes, you might get sick, but you never do."

Well, you see she had me licked. I

then said, "I may get hurt in a polo game by falling off my horse."

She said, "No, you have fallen off so much, you've got used to it, so I have no more hopes along that line."

So last summer when paying time came, and as she's the banker, my insurance man—he really shouldn't be one, he's so different from the others—advised her to reduce the policies. They decided to cut down on the accident and disability, but they allowed the straight life to remain. They figured I would die, but that I would die without illness. Well, I didn't know the thing had been cut down.

One day I was a-laying in the hospital and I just happened to have the only bright thought that had come to me in weeks. "Say, this thing I'm doubled up here with comes under the heading of 'sickness'; it even comes under the heading of 'accident,'" For wasn't I getting well from an operation?

So I thought of those policies I had been paying on for years. This sickness is going to turn out all right, at that. I began to think how I could stretch it out into what might be termed a slow convalescense. So I was grinning like a moving-picture producer who has just thought of a suggestive title to his new picture. So when my wife called again I broke the good news to her.

I says, "If we can get a bona-fide doctor to say that I have been sick and couldn't spin a rope and talk about Coolidge, we are in for some disability."

Well, I noticed the wife didn't seem so boisterous about this idea. Then I got thinking: "Maybe I haven't been sick enough, or maybe I haven't got a bona-fide doctor."

Then the truth did slowly out; she told me the sad story of the cutting down of the insurance. It read like a sentence to me. She said my physical condition had misled them. Of course she said there would be some salvage out of our short-sightedness, but that the operation would be by no means money-making. Whereas if the original policies had prevailed I would have reaped a neat benefit.

So if you want to stay well, just bet a lot of rich companies that you will get sick; then if you can't have any luck getting sick, have the policy cut down, and before six months you'll be saying "Doctor, the pain is right there."

Of course I got this consolation: If I had had the bigger policy, why, it would have had some clause in there where I got sick on the wrong day or had the wrong disease or that policy didn't cover rock quarries. There would have been an alibi somewhere, for those four pages of clauses in a policy are not put in there just to make it longer.

So I guess everything happened for the best. After all, it's not the operation that's bad; it's the caster oil afterwards. I know now how Mussolini conquered Italy.

Now I think anybody that suffers must do so with a view or purpose in mind, and that's why I want to point a moral in this yarn. When people have tonsils removed, they come out bragging about it and tell what the operation was for; the same with adenoids; and they start talking about their appendices before their wraps are off. But with Gall Bladder they never bring the name of the operation into public ear-shot. They say they have been operated on, but they don't say what for.

Now I figures out that it's the name that's against it. Now I don't know why that name should be a more offensive thing to speak of while the company is just settling down to steady scandal gossip than any other part of the body. It's just among a lot of other what the doctors call organs, and to operate on these with undesirable names should be no disgrace for conversational purposes. But it's just human nature; we always like something with some big name that we don't know anything about; some doctor for no reason at all, outside of the fee, called it the appendix. It had a nice sounding name. Now, everybody that don't know what to be operated on for, have their appendices removed.

Now the Gall Bladder means something; it's a real name of a real functioning organ, same as the heart functions— in some people. But the name is all wrong for living and dining room gossip. It's too crude, it's too sudden, it's not euphonius, it means too much what it is; it's like a toothpick—we want to use it but we don't want to let anybody know it. And as for operations, why appendices can't compare with this other.

Why, appendices are taken out just while they are looking for something else, while this other calls for a table, a lot of nurses and a bunch of ether; it's a surgeons' operation; while appendices is a hospital night-watchman's job. If we ever make it amount to anything as a

topic, we have got to change its name,
and I have been giving the name a lot of
thought. I thought we ought to call it
something from the Latin.

The word "Gaul" itself is not bad.
Gaul was a nation that flourished when
the flourishing was good, and was extin-
guished when the extinguishing was good.
So it's the second word of the disease that
makes the name objectionable. So what
you say we take the first letter of the first
name, which is G, and the first letter of
the second name, which is B, and for eu-
phonious reasons we add double E to each
one of these and tack on an S to the last
one for good measure and that gives us
the word Gee-Bee's?

Now don't get this confused with Hee-
BeeJeeBee's. What we've got or just
had are just GeeBee's. Now that name

means so little that it ought to become popular. It sounds good and has no objectionable features that I can see, and ought to give us entree anywhere. I don't want to just stand around a party and point to my scar and not be able to tell what disease put it there. This appendix crowd has lorded it over other operations long enough. Now that we've got a name with no harsh sounding words, let us GeeBee people step in and get some of the credit. Why, on account of its location we can point with much more modesty to our scars.

But I am broad-minded. I think that all operations should be on an equality. Any time you have whiffed the ether, that should make you eligible to speak publicly and call your operation by its name, no matter what region is remodeled.

If you have been overhauled, you should be eligible to enter any conversation, for you are then one of the Fraternity of Scarbellies.

So if I can lift the GeeBee's operation to the social standing in conversational circles that Appendix now occupies, then my illness will not have been in vain. Are you with me, GeeBee's? Then Scars front! Forward, march! Viva, GeeBee's!

THE END